Dear Parent:

Congratulations! Your child is taking the first steps on an exciting journey. The destination? Independent reading!

STEP INTO READING® will help your child get there. The program offers books at five levels that accompany children from their first attempts at reading to reading success. Each step includes fun stories, fiction and nonfiction, and colorful art. There are also Step into Reading Sticker Books, Step into Reading Math Readers, and Step into Reading Phonics Readers—a complete literacy program with something to interest every child.

Learning to Read, Step by Step!

Ready to Read Preschool–Kindergarten
• big type and easy words • rhyme and rhythm • picture clues
For children who know the alphabet and are eager to begin reading.

Reading with Help Preschool–Grade 1
• basic vocabulary • short sentences • simple stories
For children who recognize familiar words and sound out new words with help.

Reading on Your Own Grades 1–3
• engaging characters • easy-to-follow plots • popular topics
For children who are ready to read on their own.

Reading Paragraphs Grades 2–3
• challenging vocabulary • short paragraphs • exciting stories
For newly independent readers who read simple sentences with confidence.

Ready for Chapters Grades 2–4
• chapters • longer paragraphs • full-color art
For children who want to take the plunge into chapter books but still like colorful pictures.

STEP INTO READING® is designed to give every child a successful reading experience. The grade levels are only guides. Children can progress through the steps at their own speed, developing confidence in their reading, no matter what their grade.

Remember, a lifetime love of reading starts with a single step!

To my mother
—S.A.K.

Cover photo credits: Kareem Abdul-Jabbar (Allsport); Michael Jordan (John Biever/*Sports Illustrated*); Julius Erving (Manny Millan/*Sports Illustrated*); Wilt Chamberlain (Sheedy & Long/*Sports Illustrated*); Larry Bird (Richard Mackson/*Sports Illustrated*).

Text photo credits: Page 1: see cover photo credits, above; page 3: see cover photo credits, above; page 4: Rick Stewart/Allsport; page 6: Walter Iooss, Jr.; page 12: Sheedy & Long/*Sports Illustrated*; page 20: Allsport; page 28: Jerry Wachter/Focus on Sports; page 36: Focus on Sports; page 44: Walter Iooss, Jr./*Sports Illustrated* (Elgin Baylor); AP/Wide World Photos (Shaquille O'Neal); all others, Focus on Sports.

www.stepintoreading.com

Educators and librarians, for a variety of teaching tools, visit us at
www.randomhouse.com/teachers

Library of Congress Cataloging-in-Publication Data
Kramer, Sydelle. Basketball's greatest players / by S. A. Kramer.
    p. cm. — (Step into reading. A step 5 book)
SUMMARY: Describes how and why such men as Bill Russell, Wilt Chamberlain, and Larry Bird became great basketball players.
ISBN 0-679-88112-3 (trade) — ISBN 0-679-98112-8 (lib. bdg.)
1. Basketball players—United States—Biography—Juvenile literature. 2. Basketball players—Rating of—United States—Juvenile literature. [1. Basketball players.] I. Title.
II. Series: Step into reading. Step 5 book.
GV884.A1 K727 2003   796.323'092'2—dc21   2002013804

Printed in the United States of America   25 24 23 22 21 20 19 18

STEP INTO READING, RANDOM HOUSE, and the Random House colophon are registered trademarks of Random House, Inc.

STEP INTO READING®

BASKETBALL'S GREATEST PLAYERS

by S. A. Kramer

Random House 🏠 New York

Introduction

What's the hottest sport around? Basketball. It's 48 minutes of non-stop action. Take your eyes off the court for an instant and you'll miss a slam dunk, a behind-the-back pass, or a sneaky steal.

Basketball is the only sport completely developed in America. A Massachusetts teacher, Dr. James Naismith, invented the game with his wife's help in 1891.

Today, people shoot hoops all over the world. From college campuses to NBA (National Basketball Association) arenas, basketball keeps fans on the edge of their seats.

And nobody plays it better than the men of the NBA. Fans love to argue about who's the greatest. This book tells you all you want to know about the best players ever.

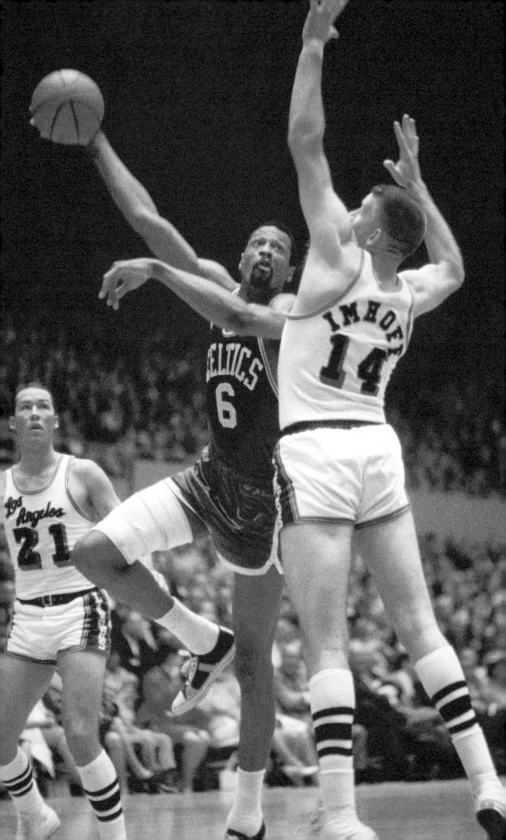

1
DEFENSE!

College ball, 1953. The game between the University of San Francisco and Brigham Young University has just started. Bill Russell, a sophomore (second-year student), is San Francisco's center. At 6'10", he can outjump everyone on the floor.

Five seconds go by. The man Bill's guarding dribbles around him. When the man goes in for an easy layup, San Francisco's captain scowls at Bill. "Why don't you try playing some defense?" he hisses.

Bill gets angry. He knows the captain doesn't like him. Bill is black and the captain is white—they sometimes clash because of that. There and then, he decides he'll show the captain exactly what defense is. He says, "I made up my mind to be a championship basketball player."

No emotion crosses Bill's face. He sticks to his man as though his life were at stake. The player doesn't score another point.

Later, Bill realizes he's proved that defense can win games. From now on, he vows, that's what he'll concentrate on.

Other centers feel defense is unimportant. If they don't have the ball, they just stand around the basket. When they block shots, they slap the ball hard into the stands.

Bill shows them a whole new way of playing. He makes defense lead to fast breaks and scoring. Timing his leaps, he tips blocked shots to teammates racing downcourt. He tears around the floor, stealing balls and grabbing rebounds.

In 1956, Bill joins the NBA. He's the Boston Celtics' only black player. His style of play singlehandedly changes basketball defense.

The league is startled when Bill doesn't care about his own statistics. He can score easily—but he won't. The Celtics don't need points from him to win. They count on him to make sure the team works together. Bill becomes the greatest team player ever.

With him in the middle, the Celtics win 11 championships in 13 years. Eight of them are in a row. No other team, in *any* sport, has accomplished such a feat.

But Bill is never very popular with the fans. A loner, he keeps his distance from almost everybody. After a while he even refuses to sign autographs. He doesn't care if he's liked—he just wants to be respected.

Not many people know the real Bill. He was born poor in a small Louisiana town. Because he was black, white kids threw rocks at him. The two races were so separate, young Bill hardly ever spoke to any whites.

When he was 12, his mother died suddenly. To this day, Bill hasn't gotten over it. But he's learned to act tough. Even in a game, he hides his true feelings. He seems calm on the court, yet he often throws up before he plays.

There's one thing Bill never hides—his pride in his race. Bill is one of the first black athletes to speak out against prejudice. The Celtics name him the first black head coach in professional sports. After his retirement, he's the first black sportscaster on national TV.

Bill may have scored fewer than 15,000 points, but his defense and team play made him a great champion. That's why, in 1980, he was named the best basketball player ever by the Professional Basketball Writers Association of America. Bill knows there's no higher honor in the game.

WILLIAM FELTON RUSSELL

(RUSS, SECRETARY OF DEFENSE)

Born 2/12/34   6'10", 220 lbs.

Played center for the Boston Celtics 1956–69

Most Valuable Player 5 times

Hall of Fame

- Second in career rebounds: 21,620
- Led the league in rebounds 4 times
- Won more championships than any other player: 11
- College team won 55 games in a row and 2 National College Athletic Association (NCAA) titles
- First player to win the MVP 3 seasons in a row
- Named best basketball player ever by the Professional Basketball Writers Association of America (1980)

2
SCORE!

Hershey, Pennsylvania. March 2, 1962. The Philadelphia Warriors and the New York Knicks are about to play one of the last games of the season.

Wilt Chamberlain, the Warriors' star center, barely notices. He's tired—he didn't get any sleep the night before. But he knows he'll do well anyway. Wilt's proud and always needs to be the best. He wraps a rubber band around his right wrist. It's his good-luck charm.

Four thousand fans have come to see Wilt play. At 7'1", he's the NBA's first giant superstar. His height and strength have changed the game forever.

Before Wilt, centers weren't much taller

than other players. They didn't weigh close to Wilt's 270 pounds. Few could control the ball and pour in the points. Now every team wants someone like Wilt—a huge scoring center who can take over the game.

Wilt is an iron man. He doesn't play as if he's bushed. In the first half alone, he scores 41 points! Sweat pours off him. As always, he changes his jersey at halftime. Then he drinks half a gallon of milk to put liquid back into his body.

In the second half, Wilt keeps piling on the points. There's no defense against his dipper dunk, which he stuffs hard through the net. No one can stop the fadeaway jumper he shoots while falling away from the hoop. He also uses the finger roll—gently sliding the ball off his fingers into the basket.

Now the game's in the fourth quarter. Wilt has over 80 points. The fans start yelling—they want him to score 100. No one has ever done it before.

The Knicks are determined to stop Wilt. They hang all over his back. They pound him with fouls. But Wilt's teammates get him the ball—and Wilt keeps scoring.

A minute to go. Wilt has 98 points. Now he's truly exhausted—he's played the entire game. Can he make one last basket? He gets the ball, shoots—and misses.

A teammate grabs the rebound and passes it back to Wilt. Wilt slips past the defense and goes in for a layup. *Swoosh!* He's scored 100 points, an NBA record that has never been broken!

Fans rush the court. The Warriors win, 169–147. Wilt escapes to the locker room, where he sits quietly on a bench. Everyone is excited, but Wilt just stares at the scoring sheet. He can't quite believe what he's done.

The game becomes a legend. Wilt has made 36 baskets and 28 free throws. He's also pulled in 25 rebounds. Some sports writers feel it's the game of the century.

Fans aren't surprised Wilt has set a record. He's been a great athlete ever since he was a teenager. By the age of 14, he was seven feet tall. His huge size made him perfect for many sports.

Back then, Wilt hated his long, skinny legs. Wherever he went, he'd try to sit down so people wouldn't stare at him. His friends called him "Dip," because he had to bend down to get through doorways.

Basketball made Wilt feel better about himself. It gave him a way to use his size. He practiced up to seven hours a day.

He was fast and could jump 50 inches straight up in the air. His hands were so big that one coach said he "handled the basketball like you or I would a grapefruit." To build up his strength, he worked out with 500-pound weights.

Wilt had a great college career at the University of Kansas. After graduating in 1959, he joined the NBA. Back then, most players were white. Wilt was black—and the biggest player of all. So every move he made was watched carefully by the fans. Experts expected any team "Wilt the Stilt" played on to be a champion. Wilt felt pressured to win right away.

He took the court and scored and rebounded at will. Between 1960 and 1973, he nearly ruled the game. Wilt led the league in rebounds 11 times and was the top scorer seven years in a row. In 1,045 games, he never once fouled out.

Yet his team won the finals only twice. Sportswriters and fans blamed Wilt—they felt he was not a team player. Wilt hogged the ball, they said. He choked making foul shots and didn't move around the court. Unlike his archrival, Bill Russell, he couldn't get his team to work together.

As he grew older, Wilt changed his game. He took fewer shots and made more of them. He passed off to teammates, who scored. In 1968, he became the only center ever to lead the league in assists. Traded from Philadelphia to the Lakers that same year, he started to play strong defense. In 1971–72, he led them to a 33-game winning streak—and the championship.

Wilt always said, "Where there's a Wilt, there's a way." He stayed fit even as he aged, running in marathons. But in 1999, he died suddenly at the age of 63. Fans will always remember him as one of basketball's greatest players.

WILTON NORMAN CHAMBERLAIN

(WILT THE STILT, THE BIG DIPPER)

Born 8/21/36   7'1", 270 lbs.

Played center for the Philadelphia (later Golden State) Warriors, Philadelphia 76ers, and Los Angeles Lakers, 1959–73

Most Valuable Player 4 times

Hall of Fame

- **First in career rebounds: 23,924**
- Most rebounds in a single game: 55
- **Most rebounds in a single season: 2,149**
- Most points scored in a single game: 100
- **Most points scored in a single season: 4,029**
- Most complete games in a single season: 79
- **Highest career rebound average: 22.9 per game**
- Highest scoring average in a single season: 50.4
- **Highest field goal percentage in a single season: .727**
- Fourth in career points: 31,419
- **Second in career scoring average: 30.1**
- Third in minutes played: 47,859
- **Most points in a rookie season: 2,707**
- Most assists by a center in a single game: 21
- **League's leading scorer most times: 7**
- Most baskets without a miss in a single game: 18
- **Most baskets in a row without a miss: 35**
- Scored 70 or more points in a game 6 times (two other players have scored 70 or more points in a game—but each of them did it only once)

3
SKYHOOK

May 10, 1974. The sixth game of the NBA finals. Fans in the Boston Garden are going wild. Their Celtics are beating the Milwaukee Bucks, 101–100, in double overtime. Just seven seconds are left in the game.

The Bucks have the ball. They know this is their last chance. Their star center, Kareem Abdul-Jabbar, grabs a pass from the sidelines. Kareem hasn't given up. No player hates to lose more.

There's no time to waste. Kareem tries to pass the ball. But his teammates near the basket are closely guarded. He's going to have to take the shot himself.

The 7'2" giant dribbles once, then turns. The clock shows three seconds. Kareem feels as if he's in slow motion. The fans are screaming, but he doesn't hear them. Players speed near him, but he sees no one. It's as though he's completely alone.

Kareem's back is to the basket. Suddenly, he leaps into the air. His right leg bends, but his left leg stays straight. With his left arm, he keeps the Celtics away. With his right arm, he raises the ball high above his head. He balances it there on his fingertips.

With a flick of his hand, Kareem guides the ball toward the hoop. The fans hold their breath—it's his famous skyhook! Kareem first made this shot in college because he wasn't allowed to dunk—he scored too many points. Whenever he shoots the skyhook, he's as graceful as a dolphin.

Now the ball drops through the basket. The net doesn't even move. Two points! The Bucks win, 102–101. Kareem lifts his arms in triumph. He's won another one for his team. Later, he says he felt "all power was mine."

But the Celtics win the next game and take the series. Fans everywhere, though, remember how Kareem won Game Six. He's always been a clutch player. For years, he's been a basketball sensation. He thrilled fans as a young boy, and he's never stopped.

Kareem was the talk of basketball by the time he reached eighth grade. His skinny body and long arms seemed meant for the sport. The taller he grew, the better he got. He was seven feet tall at the age of 14.

Young Kareem hated being famous. He was a serious student who loved music and books. Quiet and shy, he disliked attention. His greatest wish was to be the same height as his friends.

Being famous, Kareem said later, "pushed me inside myself." He learned to keep his feelings secret. On the court, he hid his emotions. Sometimes he was so calm, he looked as if he just didn't care. Fans complained he didn't play the game hard. They were wrong—Kareem wanted "to win everytime I get on the court."

And win he did. He scored and scored everywhere he played. In college, his team, UCLA, lost only two games in three years. In the NBA, he led the Bucks to one championship and the Los Angeles Lakers to five.

No one could keep Kareem away from the hoop. Season after season, he was a leader in scoring and rebounding. One of basketball's most consistent athletes, he played more years—and scored more points—than anyone else.

For most of his career, Kareem was the tallest man in the game. When opponents tried to guard him, they could never reach over him. Going for the ball, they often accidentally scratched his eyes. After his eyes were hurt for the sixth time, Kareem began to wear goggles. They made him seem even tougher on the court.

Despite his size, Kareem never pushed players around. He didn't like fighting and never talked trash. But opponents knew they'd better watch out if he lost his temper. Once he slugged a player who elbowed him hard. Kareem broke his own hand—and knocked the man unconscious.

Kareem was a superstar—yet the sport could make him anxious. To clear his mind before a game, he often read a newspaper or a book. Always the first to leave the locker room, he had trouble sleeping when he got home. Frequently, he had severe headaches called migraines.

His religion comforted him. Although he was born a Catholic, he became a Muslim in college. He dropped his old name, Lew Alcindor, and chose a new one—Kareem Abdul-Jabbar. It means noble, generous, and powerful servant of God. It was a fitting name to take with him into the record books as basketball's greatest scorer.

KAREEM ABDUL-JABBAR

(Born Ferdinand Lewis Alcindor, Jr.)

Born 4/16/47   7'2", 225 lbs.

Played center for the Milwaukee Bucks and Los Angeles Lakers, 1969–89

Most Valuable Player 6 times

Hall of Fame

- First in career points: 38,387
- Second in blocked shots: 3,189
- Second in games played: 1,560
- First in minutes played: 57,446
- First in field goals scored: 15,837
- First in field goals attempted: 28,307
- Most NBA seasons: 20
- Most seasons scoring 2,000 or more points: 9
- One of only 2 players to score over 30,000 points, grab over 10,000 rebounds, and make over 5,000 assists

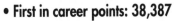

- Third in career rebounds: 17,440
- Eighth in career free throws: 6,712
- Eighth in career field goal percentage: .559
- First in personal fouls: 4,657
- Scored 1,000 or more points in 19 seasons

4
THE LEADER

Larry Bird is angry. He storms into the locker room. It's January 18, 1986, and his Boston Celtics are playing badly. At halftime, the Atlanta Hawks are crushing them by 27 points. Even worse, the Hawks and their fans seem to be laughing at the Celtics.

Larry knows his team is the best in the league. But in the past three weeks, they've gotten lazy. If someone doesn't shake them up now, they could blow their chance at the championship.

Larry snatches up a chair. He hurls it across the locker room. Then he throws another, and another. Chairs are flying all around! Soon he's screaming at his team-mates, shouting insults at them. When

Larry doesn't win, he's unhappy. Basketball is the most important thing in his life.

The Celtics don't argue with Larry. He is their leader. A forward who can shoot, pass, and rebound, he runs the team. His unselfish style makes them all better players. Many experts feel he's the best forward the game has ever seen.

When halftime is over, Larry leads his team onto the floor. He's got them fired up. If he plays well now, they'll follow.

By the end of the third quarter, he's scored 17 points. His passing is sharp—he always finds the open man. All over the court on defense, he anticipates the Hawks' every move.

Larry's play inspires the Celtics. In the fourth quarter, they make their move. They catch the surprised Hawks and win the game in overtime, 125–122. One of basketball's best team players, Larry has sparked the victory. And he's scored 41 points.

Yet back in college, few coaches expected Larry to make it in the NBA. He was a basketball hero at Indiana State, but he couldn't jump well and was often the slowest man on the floor.

The coaches didn't count on Larry's determination. Even in high school, "Basketball was all I thought about, all I wanted to do," he said. Back then, he practiced at night, on weekends, even in the rain. At 6 A.M. every school day, he'd shoot free throws for an hour and a half.

Larry loved to practice—basketball made him feel good about himself. He was a shy, skinny kid who didn't know much about the world. His family was very poor. His father had killed himself when Larry was only 19. His mother worked so hard that she was hardly ever home.

Larry learned to be careful with money. He was a neat, quiet boy at home. But on the court he was different. With a ball in his hands, he was tough and in control.

He carried his basketball everywhere. He worked on his dribbling even when he sat down! One season he broke his ankle, but insisted on practicing anyway. He learned how to pass the ball while leaning on crutches. Larry had to do everything perfectly.

In college, his points came easy. But Larry knew the NBA wouldn't be the same. So when he joined the Celtics, he always prepared carefully for a game. To warm up, he took 60 jump shots. He studied every move possible to make up for being slow. Once he took the floor, he knew where the ball was every moment of the game. His great balance and footwork made him a reliable shooter.

Larry showed how good he was right from the start. In his rookie year, he helped the Celtics achieve the *biggest* season turnaround in NBA history. The year before, the team's record had been 29–53. With Larry on board, their record improved to 61–21.

On the court, no one frightened him. He trash-talked, even to older stars. One player reported, "He'd always say, 'In your face' or 'You can't guard me.' Whatever he could use to throw you off balance."

No athlete had more confidence—he *knew* he could make the winning shot. His passing was fearless—he'd hit a man 80 feet downcourt. While Larry was a Celtic, the team won three NBA crowns.

Larry retired from basketball a wealthy

man. But to this day, he hasn't changed his habits. He watches his money carefully. Friends joke he'll dive to the floor for a nickel. Ever the perfectionist, he's so neat that his mother calls him "Mr. Clean." He still wants to win so badly, he gets mad when he loses at Ping-Pong.

When he wasn't playing basketball, Larry could seem clumsy. Even now, he can't manage to knot his own tie. But his hands were sure and steady whenever they had the ball.

He brought his winning ways to coaching in 1997. With the Indiana Pacers, Larry was named Coach of the Year his very first season. By 2000, he had taken the team to the NBA finals.

That same year, Larry retired again. He's left his mark on his sport, both as player and as coach.

LARRY JOE BIRD

(HICK FROM FRENCH LICK,
LARRY LEGEND)

Born 12/7/56   6'9", 220 lbs.

**Played forward for the
Boston Celtics, 1979–92**

Most Valuable Player 3 times

Hall of Fame

- Fifth in free throw percentage: .886
- Led league in free throw percentage 4 times
- Made 71 free throws in a row
- One of 5 players to score over 20,000 total points
  and have over 5,000 total assists
- In 1985–86, finished in the top ten in scoring,
  rebounding, steals, free throw percentage,
  and three-point shooting percentage—
  one of the greatest seasons ever

5
THE GREATEST

Michael Jordan has a dream. More than anything, he wants to make his high school basketball team. He's only in the tenth grade, but already he's 5'11". A terrific athlete, he thinks he can pass the tryout.

If he makes the team, he'll feel better about himself. Right now, he's very insecure. Kids tease him about his haircut. They poke fun at the way his ears stick out. When he shoots hoops, his friends laugh because his tongue hangs out.

Michael goes to the tryout. Two weeks later, a list goes up. He can't wait to see the list. But he doesn't want to read it alone. With a friend by his side, he says, "I looked and looked for my name."

It isn't there. Michael feels numb. When he gets home, he says, "I went to my room and I closed the door and I cried."

But he doesn't give up. He hates being disappointed. When summer comes, he practices basketball every day.

By the time school starts, Michael has grown more than four inches. His new height makes it easier for him to score. Practice has helped him understand how the game should be played. When he tries out for the team this time, he makes it. All his hard work has paid off.

Michael's a good high school player. But not even his friends think he'll make it to the NBA. Only a few colleges want him to play for their teams. But the University of North Carolina decides to take a chance. And Michael erases all doubt with just one shot.

It's 1982, during his first year at the

university. He's a skinny guard for the Tar Heels, the basketball team. They're playing in the NCAA (National Collegiate Athletic Association) final. With just seconds to go, they're one point behind.

Seventeen feet from the hoop, Michael gets the ball. The Tar Heels' chance at the championship is now in his hands.

He coolly takes a jump shot. He looks as if he's sure it's going in. And it does! He's won the game. His basket is nicknamed "The Shot." Michael is an instant star. Throughout his college years, he gets better and better. In 1984, he joins the NBA's Chicago Bulls. He wins the scoring crown in his rookie year.

Whenever he has the ball, he seems unstoppable. He can get shots off anytime— three-pointers, reverse layups, over-the-shoulder jams. No one looks as fast. No one jumps as high. Michael can even make foul shots with his eyes closed!

Soon everyone in America wants to see Michael Jordan play. They gasp when he leaps and seems to hang in the air. Tongue out, he floats to the basket as though he'll never come down. When he flies toward the hoop, he can shift the ball from hand to hand. It never slips because his hands are so gigantic.

Michael's a skilled passer and rebounder who also plays superb defense. He rarely feels tired. His arms and legs are strong from lifting weights. And when the Bulls need a basket, he always gets the ball. He says, "I love it when it comes down to that one moment and it's all in my hands."

He's a nice guy off the court—but watch out when he's got the ball. When he talks trash to opponents, they don't usually talk back. No one wants to get Michael angry. He plays even *better* when he's mad.

Experts quickly recognize Michael as the greatest basketball player ever. He leads the Bulls to three NBA titles in a row. His talent and charm make him the world's most popular athlete. Michael turns basketball into the sport everyone wants to play.

The game makes him a millionaire. But he doesn't become a snob. He still cleans his own house and mends his own clothes. Without bragging about it, he starts a foundation for needy children. He wears a pair of sneakers only once, giving them away to kids after each game.

Then, in 1993, his father is murdered. He was Michael's best friend. Michael is overwhelmed with grief. Suddenly, basketball doesn't seem important anymore.

Michael retires. He plays baseball for a

while. But it's not his sport—he was born for basketball. So in 1995 he returns to the Bulls. Fans everywhere welcome him back.

He hasn't lost a step. From 1996 through 1998, he leads Chicago to three more NBA championships. Twice he is voted MVP. Still the best player on the court, he retires again in 1999.

But Michael can't stay away. In 2000, he buys part of the Washington Wizards. He also becomes president of their basketball operations. Then, in 2001, he puts on a uniform again. Playing with his team, he says, is the best way to teach them how to win.

His last game is in 2003. But fans suspect that Michael won't be able to stay away. Whether as a player, coach, executive, or owner, he'll be back in basketball soon.

MICHAEL
JEFFREY JORDAN

(MICHAEL MIRACLE, AIR JORDAN, RUBBER BAND MAN, HIS AIRNESS)

Born 2/17/63   6'6", 216 lbs.

Played guard for the Chicago Bulls, 1984–93, 1995–98, then for the Washington Wizards, 2001–2003

Most Valuable Player 5 times

- First in all-time scoring average
- Has won the NBA scoring title more than anyone else—10 times
- Has scored 10 points or more in 487 games in a row (the longest, highest scoring streak ever)
- Holds the playoff scoring record: 63 points in one game
- One of only 5 players to score 50 or more points in a finals game
- First player ever to be named the finals MVP 3 years in a row—and he did it twice for a total of 6 awards
- Has the highest scoring average ever in finals games: 41 points
- Named to the NBA All-Defensive First Team 6 times in a row, 9 times altogether
- Scored 25,000 points faster than any other player except Wilt Chamberlain
- One of only 2 players to score over 3,000 points in a single season (Chamberlain is the other)
- Only player to ever block more than 100 shots and make over 200 steals in a single season
- Third in all-time scoring

Elgin Baylor

Oscar Robertson

Shaquille O'Neal

Jerry West

Julius Erving

Earvin Johnson, Jr.

6
MORE GREATS

Bill, Wilt, Kareem, Larry, and Michael—they're the top players in basketball history. But other athletes have achieved greatness, too, changing the game of basketball with their superb skills. Here are a few of them.

Elgin Baylor was basketball's first great jumper. Hanging in the air, he scored in ways no one had seen before. Opponents could never tell whether he'd shoot or pass. Elgin's teammates nicknamed him "Motormouth," since he always seemed to be talking. He was easy to spot on the court—as he flew to the basket, his head twitched uncontrollably. Fourth-highest career scoring average—27.4. Played 1958–72.

Jerry West was such a physical guard, he broke his nose eight times, his hand three times, and his thumb once. Superb in the clutch, he was one of the most consistent scorers ever. He could shoot from anywhere on the court. During a game he showed his emotions easily. Teammates called him "Tweety Bird" because of his skinny legs, long arms, and high voice. Played 1960–74.

Oscar Robertson ("The Big O") was the NBA's first big guard. At 6'5" he was a strong, physical player who avoided flashy moves. A great believer in the basics of the game, Oscar "killed you with fundamentals." He was so committed to perfection, he'd scream at teammates if they made a mistake. The top high school and college player of his time, he could pass, shoot, dribble, and rebound. Played 1960–74.

Julius   Erving ("Dr.   J") was   the original slam dunker and the first player to dazzle fans with his leaps. As graceful as a dancer, he was so exciting to watch, opposing players forgot about the game and kept their eyes on him. He had hundreds of moves, and no one could tell which he'd make when. That helped him score over 30,000 points. He is one of only two players to score over 30,000 points, grab over 10,000 rebounds, *and* make over 5,000 assists. An electrifying forward, he changed the style of the game. Played in both the ABA (American Basketball Association), 1971–76, and the NBA, 1976–87.

Earvin ("Magic") *Johnson, Jr.,* was almost as famous for his smile as he was for his skill. He brought enthusiasm and emotion to the game, along with a talent for seeing everything on the court. At 6'9", he was a quick, tall guard who controlled the rhythm of a game. He could pass the ball as if he had eyes in the back of his head. A great team player, he led the Lakers to five championships. Along the way, he picked up three MVP awards. Larry Bird once called him "the perfect player." Diagnosed as HIV-positive (HIV is the virus that causes AIDS) in 1991, he retired from basketball, came back in 1996, then retired again. Played 1979–91, 1996.

Shaquille ("Shaq") ***O'Neal,*** at 7'1" and more than 300 pounds, is one of basketball's biggest men. He's also one of its strongest— his slam dunks shatter backboards and break goals. Years from retiring, he's the youngest player to be named one of the 50 greatest in NBA history. A three-time finals MVP, he's made the Lakers three-peat NBA champs. Started playing in 1992.